Messages From The Mountain

CW01096197

AMANDA GOLDSTON

Copyright notice

First published in the UK in 2022 by Amanda Goldston
© Amanda Goldston 2022

ISBN: 978-1-908253-39-2

A CIP catalogue record for this book is available from the British Library

DEDICATION

To all the fabulous mountains where I have walked, enjoyed amazing views and transformed myself.

MY INSPIRATION FOR MESSAGES FROM THE MOUNTAIN

I am Amanda Goldston and I love traveling and walking, especially in areas where there are mountains and other stunning scenery.

I grew up in the beautiful South West of England, where wild moorlands meet dramatic coasts.

My passion for walking and mountains really began in 2014 when I won a trip to LAAX in Switzerland. I felt so at home and so at peace in the presence of the Mountains.

In 2016 I completed a Walk 1000 Miles in a Year Challenge and took myself up as many mountains and high peaks as I could in the UK.

I have a great passion for reaching the highest point that I possibly can. Standing there, taking in the Pure WOW of the breath-taking views is the most wonderful, exhilarating feeling of being alive.

I am always on the look out for a special mountain cafe where I can enjoy a refreshing cup of tea and savour some delicious local cake.

I was inspired to write this book after going on my dream hiking tour in the Swiss Alps and the Italian Dolomites.

As I walked all the old pain of the past, that was stopping me from living my best life, came surging to the surface for me to face, along with these wonderful messages of guidance.

In the presence of these Majestic Mountains, I underwent quite a personal transformation from treating myself like a Worthless Slave to living as the Powerful Queen that I am – as majestic as a Mountain. ← *Radiant*

That wonderful guidance has become this book with the title of "Messages from the Mountain."

Please feel free to take a deep breath and to open the book at any page and see what guidance is there for you.

Although this book is not a Journal, many of the messages have space for you to write your own inspiration and Messages from the Mountain.

At the end of this book are three longer Messages – Mountain You, Queen and Peace - which I have included exactly as I downloaded them and wrote them down.

They are a summary of a lot of the shorter messages and pull together all the Wisdom and Messages from a Mountain.

Whilst those messages are personal to me, my journey, my dreams and my desires, the themes of those Messages are timeless wisdom that everyone can enjoy.

My dream is to Live and Walk in the Mountains in the Wonderful Joy of Radiant Mountain Walking Girl, with vibrant health, time freedom and plenty of money to support me.

That may not be your dream, so please take the words of the Messages and apply them to you, your own life and your own dreams.

Let the Mountain support you in bringing to fruition whatever you desire.

Please enjoy this book and I trust that these Messages inspire and uplift you as much as they have done for me.

MESSAGES FROM THE MOUNTAIN

Insignificant Problems

All problems become very small and insignificant in the presence of a mountain. It puts things into perspective. Give all your problems to the mountains and let them dissolve into nothing.

Let go of all the small-minded thinking and trying to figure things out for yourself. Allow yourself to receive bigger and more expansive solutions.

Ask yourself – "How can I become as Mighty as a Mountain in the presence of that problem?"

Priorities

Come to the Mountains for your own Joy and your own Peace and not because you are following another person and their dreams.

Important

It is time to focus on what you care about and not let the noise take over your brain.

Wonderful

Look with Wonder at that which is around you.

The simple phrase of "WOW! Isn't it Wonderful! Thank you" is immensely powerful to change your whole day. Repeat it often, breathe into it, smile and let out a sigh of satisfaction.

Live in the joyful knowing and positive expectation that Something Wonderful is Happening to You today.

Have your plan and be open to letting the Mountain surprise, delight and WOW you.

Flow

Move with Ease and Flow, let everything be easy. Don't worry and fret and just enjoy the flow of the day.

Be open to the Ease of Everything. Expect it to be easy, notice when it is easy and be grateful for the ease.

Openness

Be open to the wonderful joy of the day and the magic of new experiences. Enjoy each moment of the day, whatever it brings.

Sit in Pleasure and fun and be open to new experiences. Have no expectations of anyone or anything. Just let them be what they are and enjoy them for what they are.

Breathe, savour the moment as every moment is beautiful, take it all in, be WOW-ed at every step and every turn.

Who am I?

Who do I truly want to be? Let the Mountain support you to become the person of your dreams and desires. Become as big and majestic as a mountain.

The Mountains offer you the opportunity to be the most joyful and most expansive person you can be.

New You

You cannot take any part of the old woman with you, you have to leave the old self completely behind you to be born again, so there is no trace of the old.

Define yourself anew as the person you truly desire to be and begin to live as that new person. Life from the state of the new person.

Rise up to who you are. Be the biggest, most joyful version of yourself. Celebrate your bigness, celebrate the vastness of you.

Be rooted in the Earth and rise up, tall, solid and immovable in who you are.

Nobody messes with the Mountain. The Mountain is timeless - no past, no future, just the rock-solid groundedness of the now, present moment.

Changes

Nothing is ever lost, there are only things that need to fall away so something better can come into your life. Don't mourn what seems to be lost or changing, celebrate its passing and open yourself up to something new and bigger.

The old has to break down and fall away for the space to be made for the new to reveal itself and to be formed.

When the old breaks away, it reveals the secrets of the true Essence that are hidden beneath the old layers.

Breakdown has to precede Breakthrough.

When Glaciers break and the shape of the mountains alters, it gives man and scientists more information to learn about the mountain and what is going on.

Past

Don't try to change the past. It was what it was, it happened for your growth. Be grateful for it, be grateful for what happened and for the people involved and move into a more expanded space to welcome in new things and people.

Let Go

Let go of feelings of lack and what is missing in your life and focus on the blessings that are here now.

Focus on who you desire to be and the Wonderful Joy that is found everywhere around you right now. Let it be easy. Trust and expect a miracle.

Wild

How Wild it Was to Let it Be!

Have your dreams and desires and then let it all unfold in the most natural way. Don't try to control it, just be open to the magic that is on its way to you and follow the next right step that you are guided to do.

Present

Forget the past, the future is not here yet, so stop worrying and fretting about it. Enjoy the present moment now, feel the wonderful joy of who you are now in this present moment.

Reason

There is always a reason why something happens and everything is always perfect, even if you can't see it in the moment. Be prepared for the clouds to part and for something better to appear for you.

Nothing is good or bad, it just is. Take away judgement and meaning and just notice what shows up. Treat everything with wonder and curiosity.

The journey to your dream is rarely a straight line, there are ups and downs so take it all in your stride, one step at a time.

Gifts

Find a gift and a learning in every experience. Things happen FOR you and your growth and not TO you.

Talk to everyone and listen to everyone. Let people be who they are, don't judge others and see what gift every person has for you.

Resistance

Every moment is leading you to your desired dream, even if it does not seem like it right now. Don't resist what is showing up right now, just be open and go with it and see what shows up next.

Unfold

Let go, stop trying so hard to make things happen. Let it unfold naturally and stay in the feeling of the end.

Big Dream

Hold onto your big dream and share it where appropriate and look for the wonderful joy in each passing moment.

You never know who might be able to help you. A chance conversation could change the course of your life forever.

End

Speak and feel your desire. Focus FROM the END, then trust, let go, know and feel that It Is Done. Thank you.

Stay grounded in the feeling of who you desire to be. Take the steps you are guided to make, even if they make no logical sense and expect the money, resources and people to show up for everything you need.

Creativity

Let the Creative ideas flow and allow the appropriate help to come to you to create it. Focus on your strengths, ideas and creativity and seek help for all the rest of it.

Let the ideas flow downwards as inspiration from the heavens and ground them into the earth, then take action - from idea to reality.

Inspiration

When inspiration for action pops into your head, stop, pause, take note of it, be grateful for the idea and then take action on it as soon as you can.

Trust

Trust yourself and your own judgement. Don't just follow the crowd. Just because the crowd is moving in a particular direction doesn't mean they know where they are going or it is good for you.

Instinct

Trust that immediate, first instinct. Don't second guess yourself, even when it seems illogical to the mind.

Simple

Keep it simple, one step at a time. Get started, don't wait until it is perfect or you will wait forever. You can course correct as you go along. A small amount of something is better than a large amount of nothing.

One Thing

Don't put too much into your day. Do the ONE most important and most enjoyable thing FIRST, ~~plan to~~ complete that with as much fun and pleasure as possible and then, if you have time, add on something else that is also pleasurable and fun.

One thing at a time, thoroughly enjoyed is better than lots of things rushed.

Risks

Don't be afraid to start over, to go for your dreams, to take a chance, a risk and a leap of faith. Just go for it and let the Mountain support you.

New Things

Try something new. Don't be afraid, it will probably be easier and more fun than you first thought. Laugh at yourself if you don't get it 100% perfect 1st time.

One Step

Take a step towards your dreams and the Mountain will take a step - or maybe several towards you.

You make the 1st move, trust the next step and the Mountain supports you and moves towards you.

Stop fretting over how it is going to happen, relax and trust that the next right step will show up with ease.

Strength

You are stronger than you think you are and you can accomplish more than you think you can as long as you take it all one step at a time.

Powerful

Realise how powerful you are. Your wish is my command.

Light

Be the Light, the Sunshine and the Radiant, Shining Sparkle Star that you are. Enjoy the Ease and Flow of one foot in front of another, one step at a time.

Joy

Today I experience the Pure Pleasure and
wonderful joy of the Radiant I am and enjoy
every step and every breath of the way. BEING

Pleasure and Turn On

Follow the Pleasure and the Turn On. Follow your passions and your bliss, follow what energises you, inspires you and turns you on to the juice of life.

How

Notice if you are feeling sadness, frustration or stuckness. That is often you caught in trying to figure out the HOW when you are not seeing your dream come to pass.

Focus on the Joy and Gratitude of your desire being realised and Let it BE!

Well

Feel the sense of freedom and love and know that "All is Well."

People

Let go of people who are not at the same energy as you. You can't bring them up to a higher adventure playground unless they are willing to come with you and play. If not leave them to their own journey.

Don't shrink yourself to fit the smallness of others.

Be patient with other people. Everyone is on their own journey and going at their own pace. Don't rush them and don't be rushed by them.

Speak Up

Speak up when something needs to be said. Speak your truth in a kindly way and firm way. Your truth and voice matters.

Don't be afraid of offending other people. Offense can only be taken, not given, and if someone takes offense then that is their issue not yours.

A Mountain does not care what people think of her or say about her. She remains true to herself.

Personal

Don't take things personally. People are what they are and everyone is on their own journey.

Silence from another person or them not returning your calls or messages does not mean anything and is about them and their issues and has nothing to do with you.

If they have taken umbrage at something you have said or done and they don't tell you what upset them, you could waste a lifetime trying to guess your alleged crime. Don't bother.

If they don't want your awesomeness in their life, that is their loss. Wish them love and good will on their journey and move on.

Experience

Don't listen to the fearful nay-sayers telling you all the reasons why it can't be done.

Listen only to those who have done what you want to do, check things out for yourself, trust your own wisdom and take a chance, take your own measured risks.

It might be foggy and rainy when you start out, trust and expect it will clear up and you can enjoy your day as planned.

Positive

Choose to surround yourself with people who are joyful, expansive, supportive, fun, positive, creative, uplifting and encouraging, who enjoy pleasure, fun and laughter and who understand you and accept you for who you are.

Seek out souls who are honest, open, truthful, delightful, independent, adventurous free spirits.

Team

The Road to Success is Easy when you have the encouragement of a supportive team.

Compliments

Rise up and lift someone else up with a genuine compliment. Watch them smile and light up.

Self - Love

Fall in Love yourself and with Life so you can go your own way without having to sell yourself out to the dreams of another person.

You have got to love yourself first before you can draw in love from another person.

Follow your passions and your heart-felt bliss, enjoy the moment of today, smile, have fun and don't worry about tomorrow.

Gratitude

Smile and be grateful that you are following your heart and your dreams.

True Self

Be yourself and to thine own self be true. Love yourself for who you are and accept that who you are does not always fit into someone else's picture of who they think you should be.

Don't compromise or change yourself for someone else.

They can bend around you or better still, surround yourself with people who share your passions and who love you for who you are, without trying to change you.

Eccentric

Banish the words "sane, sensible and normal." Those who hike and climb mountains are often called weird and eccentric by those who do not understand the pull of the mountain, the challenge of the journey and the joy of the ultimate success.

Proudly embrace your inner "weird eccentric" and don't bother trying to fit in with the boring crowd, who either have no dreams, are too frightened to pursue their dreams or have given up on their dreams and life.

Respect

Be the Sovereign, Regal, Majesty, Mighty Queen Mountain of a Being that you are. Treat yourself with Respect and others will respect you.

You Decide

Go your own way, make your own choices, don't wait for other people - you decide! Make your plans, take action, let others join you if they wish to, but blaze your own trail and don't wait for them.

Adventure

Go forth on your next adventure, treat each day as an exciting voyage of discovery with the words:

"I wonder what amazing, wonderful things are coming my way today. Something wonderful is happening to me now, thank you."

Imagination

Thoroughly enjoy and savour your dream in your imagination with all your senses first, as the reality of experiencing it may not live up to your expectations, so you cannot be disappointed.

By the same token, it could always turn out even better than you could have possibly imagined.

Fewer People

The higher up you go, the less noise, the less busyness and the fewer the people there are.

The more effort is required, the fewer people will be there and the better the view.

Look for the little gondolas and cable cars as they will most likely have more of the local people savouring the views that are off the beaten track.

Slow Down

Slow down, don't rush, take your time, go at the pace of the Majestic, Regal Mountain – which is slow and measured - and savouring every moment of the journey. Pause and enjoy the views as you go along.

The Journey itself often brings more joy and WOW moments than rushing to the final destination.

Silence

Relish the sound of silence, stop every so often to take in the silence, ground your feet in the Earth and feel the power of the Earth. Breathe deeply and slowly. Breathe in the silence.

Be silent and let Joy seep through your whole being, as your senses come alive. Let yourself be inspired by Silence.

Challenge and Rest

Challenge yourself and rest when you need to, listen to your body. Have a regular Reality Check of weather, safety and how your body is feeling.

Don't think you have to keep up with others and don't bow to the pressure to over-exert yourself. Honour yourself and rest as you need to.

Don't be afraid to speak up in a group if you want to go faster and you want more challenge and slower if you need to slow down.

Pace

Go at your own pace, stop when you you are struggling. There is rarely strength in pushing through something as that can often lead to exhaustion and collapse.

Seek help where and when you need it. If you are going to really challenge yourself, make sure you know what you are doing, you are properly prepared with the right equipment for the job and seek professional help and guidance if you need it.

Seek out people who have done what you want to do. Be careful who you take advice from, make sure they are competent and know what they are doing.

Stop, pause, breathe, regroup and do what you can for today as tomorrow is another day for you to take the next step. Walk until you are physically exhausted and then, when you need to rest and sleep, do that.

When the heavy rain comes and the clouds gather, go indoors and rest. You can pick up where you left off tomorrow.

The Mountain will be here for another day.

Body

Go with your body feeling. If something does not feel right and does not feel grounded in truth, walk away.

The more you ground your feet into the Earth, the more you feel your truth in your body.

Feet

Trust your feet and your body to guide you, they know what they are doing, so look up and ahead.

The faster pace you walk at, the more energised and less tired you feel. Walk at the pace of your Essence. Skipping, Dancing and Jumping down a Mountain is like gliding down on a comfortable chair and is much more efficient.

Looking down at your feet often causes you to trip over.

Connection

Connect your feet with the earth and open your heart and mind to new possibilities, love yourself and this moment and feel the joy and gratitude of pleasure, freedom and being loved, supported and nourished.

Smile and enjoy every step.

Path

Trust there is a path, even if you can't actually see it, take the next few steps or even the next single step forward that you can see and the path will open up and become clear to you.

Grounding

Root and Ground yourself and your desires into the Earth as you walk so you really connect yourself with the land, really breathe in and take in the smell of the land.

Nature

The power of nature is a force to be reckoned with - handle with care and respect - yet it is also incredibly energising and rejuvenating.

Prepared

Be prepared for all weathers as it can change in an instant in the Mountains.

Whilst the weather forecast may say Rain, Thunder & Lightning, put on your suncream and expect a dry, sunny day.

Mountains

Mountains are Queens.

They have a changeless, timeless, wonderful appeal. Each one is uniquely gorgeous in her quirkiness, steadfast, independent, often challenging and yet exuding a calm, supportive, patient air of peace.

Mountains are loved and lovely, a source of wonderful, joyful fun and endless enjoyment.

They are strong, powerful and proud, a natural, living breathing source of life and growth, open to the elements and at one with all the lifeforce that supports them and is supported by them.

People tread all over them and they stand firm, unwavering, non-resistant, grounded and rock-solid strong and are completely unmoved.

People try to conquer and tame them and the Mountain is always the stronger.

Mountains are respected, revered and honoured.

They are mighty and majestic, perfectly balanced in their imperfections, attractive, and pleasurable, yet can have an enigmatic, moody presence as they rise up and tower above the world.

Companion

You are never lonely when you have a mountain as your constant companion.

New Heights

The Mountain will always take you to new heights that you previously thought you could not reach.

Set your sights on the mountain top, and then go to the next one.

Magnitude

Sometimes you can only see so far, to what you think is the mountain top. When you get there, you see the next point that looks like the top.

If you could see the whole journey to the top, from the bottom, you probably would not start because you would be overwhelmed by the magnitude of the task, so go as far as you can see and then see what is beyond that.

Hiding

In the silence of the mountain, insights and bare truth presents themselves. You cannot hide from a mountain or from yourself in the presence of a mountain.

She calls you to be the greatest version of yourself and nothing less is acceptable.

Escapism

Find Joy and Peace in the Mountains, don't push yourself to extreme walking, just to escape from pain.

Let the pain flow through you as you walk and release it to the Earth.

Clouds

When the clouds are around a mountain, she can be considered to be moody, much like a woman expressing her emotions.

Approach with Caution, Respect and Reverence.

Treat a Mountain – or a Woman - with respect when she has dark clouds around her, as there is probably something much deeper going on than shows on the surface.

Honour and respect her and she will protect and support you. Dishonour and Disrespect her and she'll bite you and might even destroy you.

Freedom

Mountains are freedom of heart and mind and body and soul. Mountains are new adventures and new challenges.

Mountain Hiking and Exploration is Freedom and there is room on the path for everyone, whatever pace they are going at.

Mountain You

Dream your biggest dream, plant your roots firmly in the conviction of your dream and the conviction of who you are, create your solid base and rise up, be open and share what needs to be shared and keep private what needs to be kept private.

Be vast, truthful and honest. Be open for everyone to see who you are, to see you stand in your power and your majesty.

People don't conquer you, they raise you up with their support and attention. Each time someone looks at you with awe and reverence, you are an inspiration to them to reach higher and to rise up to their own dreams.

Each time they look at you with wonder, it raises them up and it raises you up.

Look with Wonder at that which is before you.

Be the mountain that is the inspiration to others. No Ego is required. Your majestic mountain being and presence is more than enough to inspire others and lift them up.

Blaze the trail up your own mountain and leave a trail of guiding light for others to follow up their own mountain. ~~and~~ Everyone will have their own path up their own personal mountain.

Become and embrace the majestic mountain bigness of who you are and your dreams.

No dream is too big and no mountain is too huge. Mountains are not obstacles, they are unrealized dreams that you need to embrace one step at a time.

There are always new heights to every mountain beyond what you can see. Grow into the majestic, regal being of power who commands respect and reverence with her quiet stillness and strength.

A mountain needs no explanation and no apology. It just is. Strong, beautiful, majestic and a challenge. Many have tried to break and conquer a mountain but the mountain is always stronger.

The mountain will keep tugging at your heart until you follow your passions and follow your biggest dream and become the biggest, most expansive, most joyful version of yourself without apology.

A mountain does not apologise and does not shrink for anyone.

Open your heart, wear your heart on your sleeve - be open and welcoming, yet be a mystery and enigmatic, be full of joyful surprises and delights.

Be strong, be guided, know that you are protected, connect with the Earth and the ground, look forward to where you are going, trust your feet to know the steps to take. Look ahead and up, not down.

Remember to look back at where you have come from and marvel at how far you have come in such a short space of time.

Mountains are before you, behind you and all round you, quietly and majestically supporting you, encouraging you and championing you.

Don't mess with a Mountain - you'll lose!!

Joyfully respect a mountain, marvel at her wonders and she will reward you with untold delights. Treat a mountain with reverence and respect, trust her and she will support you - much like a woman.

Take your time, don't rush, slow down and savour the scents and gifts along the way. Go at the pace of the mountain - slow, measured, and unhurried.

Go at the pace of the Majestic, Regal Queen that you are. A graceful Queen never hurries or rushes and the world waits for her.

Mountain Walking Girl

So who is the Amanda Mountain Walking Girl?

She is light, joyful, wonderful, smiling, grounded, rooted, strong, confident, powerful, self - assured, expansive with a strong sense of freedom.

She is healthy, independent, fearless in going for her dreams, a creative, imaginative Radiant Queen.

Who are You?

Queen

A Mountain is a regal, sovereign Queen who respects herself and commands respect wherever she is, wherever she goes and from whomsoever she comes into contact with.

Be the bold, majestic, sovereign Queen Mountain that you are and treat yourself with 1st class respect. Treat yourself like the Queen you are and everyone will respect you.

No-one treats a mountain like an unimportant, insignificant creature because a mountain does not treat herself that way. Anyone who disrespects a mountain pays the price.

People will treat you the same way you treat yourself. They cannot treat you any better or worse than you treat yourself, so treat yourself as the Sovereign, Wealthy, Powerful Queen you are.

When you are a Sovereign Queen Rich BITCH -
"Beauty in Total Control of Herself", you
command the world. You are not at the mercy
and beck and call of anyone else. You call the
shots, you command the world and the world
responds accordingly.

A Sovereign Queen is not needy or desperate
for the love and affection of others. A Queen
adores, reveres, worships and respects herself.

A Queen treats herself as she would wish
others to treat her. A Queen does not give up
her Majestic Sovereignty to please others and
to bow to their wishes or their will.

A Queen is not a worthless slave and is not
controlled by the whims of worthless slaves. A
Queen stands tall and proud and above it all.

A Queen does not accept unpleasant behaviour

from others because she does not treat herself that way.

A Queen looks after her body, mind and spirit and keeps them clean and clear.

A Queen lets other people Be who they are and stands in her own power. A Queen is true to herself. A Queen has grace and dignity and couldn't care less what others say about her or think about her.

She is not bothered and totally unfazed by the opinions of others about her. She does not let it into her awareness because it is not her truth.

A Queen walks away from unpleasant people and nasty behaviour. She does not engage with it unless it is really necessary. She simply rises above it like an eagle and proudly walks away like a snow leopard and leaves people to wallow in their own unsavoury situations of their own making.

She expects the best and expects to be treated in the finest way because she treats herself in the finest way. She forgives herself for treating herself like rubbish in the past and does not do that again.

A wealthy, powerful, sovereign Queen stands by herself in her own power and majesty and creates her own world. She fashions her world as 1st class luxury to suit herself.

A wealthy, powerful, sovereign Queen commands matter and matter responds.

A Queen is never ignored. She walks into a room and the whole room feels her presence. She lights up a room as the Sunshine and Star that she is.

She shines her light brightly into the world to

light her own way and to light the way for others to see their own magnificent, radiant beauty and Queendom.

She does not put others down, but lights the way for them to find their own magnificence.

She is fearless in pursuing her own truth, power, beauty and radiance.

She has presence and takes up all the space she needs to shine her light and beauty out into the world, completely unconcerned by the opinions of others.

Money

Money needs to be as much ease and joy and fun and pleasure as hiking in the mountains. Follow your joy and your passion, keep going with your plans in joy and pleasure and trust that the next sums of money will come, without needing to sell yourself out to a man for money.

Peace

Let go of your anger, be at peace with everyone and everything. Let people and things be as they are. That is their path, not yours. You have called them into your life for your growth and for your peace.

Learn from them. It is all FOR you and not happening TO you. As Shakespeare said, "All the world is a stage and the men and women are but players on the stage."

Let go of the old, be open to the new. Be the blank, empty canvas.

A mountain just is. It is always the same, yet every person views it in a different way, depending on where they are on their journey.

She, the Mountain does not change. The daily people and daily experiences of her might change, but she, like the soul, is eternal.

Be open and be neutral and be at peace. Face each challenge one step at a time.

Know your end destination and feel in your heart and body that you have already accomplished it. Know it is done and completed, feel the joy and celebration of completion.

Let the Mountain surprise you with both her twists and turns and with her sometimes surprising direct routes and short cuts.

Let go of the fear and the nonsense that no-one will be interested in you, your voice, your words, your creations, your books and the Messages from the Mountain and all the things you give life to in the world.

You have a voice that matters and needs to be

heard.

Let go of the old patterns and beliefs of the past, that things and hard and difficult and that you have to try to force people to like you. You absolutely don't have to do that.

Share your wisdom from the Mountain. It is old wisdom, timeless, deep, profound and a gentle reminder to people wherever they are to live in joy and pleasure and to live in the moment of now, to savour the moment of now and stop ruminating on the past and stop worrying about the future.

Live in the moment of now in wonder, joy and pleasure. Be the radiant Being you truly are.

People have told you that you inspire them just by by being who you are and by living your best life.

Embrace and accept the truth of that.

When you live in your own joy, following your passions, you automatically give other people permission to be who they are, to follow their dreams and to live their best life.

Life can change, or even end, quite dramatically in an instant. The Now present moment is all we have, savour it, breathe it, enjoy it.

Have your dreams and a destination in mind and be open and ready for it to change for the better, sometimes quite dramatically, in an instant.

Be the mountain, solid and stable, rooted and grounded, and yet reaching high up into the sky, welcoming all the weather and being all of it - the earth, the moon, the sunshine and the stars.

Glowing and basking in the light of the sunshine

and twinkling under the light of the stars.

Stop pushing and forcing. Enjoy the moment and live in wonderful joy. Be the radiant mountain you are and tower above the pettiness and silly nonsense of other people.

Be the eagle who soars on the mountain tops with a view of the whole world below, where everything is in perspective and seems so small and insignificant below.

Rise and soar and the higher you go, the fewer people there are up there in the clear mountain skies above the clouds in the valleys.

Rise above it all, be open and receptive and soar with a smile.

Talk to people and approach them with "What can I learn from them and what gift of wisdom do they have for me?" not "What can I get from them?" or "How can they help me with my plans?"

Be open and curious about the gifts from people and the gifts from the Mountain and from the day.

How can YOU be even more the shining sunshine and bright sparkling star that you already are?

Inner Mountain

Stay connected to your inner mountain. She is always there for you and always accessible as a source of strength and wisdom, even when you are not physically located in mountains.

Presence

Mountains have a voice and an individual personality and so do you. Mountains inspire people just by their presence and their being and so do you.

Contact details

Website: amandagoldston.com

Email: amandagoldston@gmail.com

Find me on Social Media:

Facebook – Amanda K G Goldston

Instagram: @MountainWalkingGirl

Printed in Great Britain
by Amazon

84643654R00058